SAILING for kids

Tim Davison & Steve Kibble

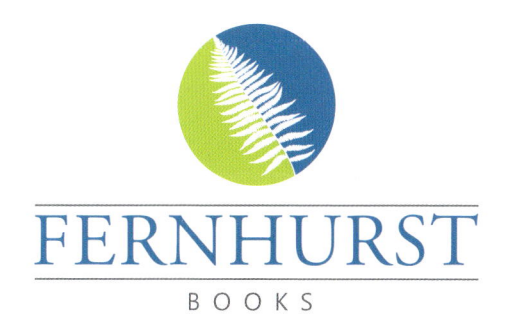

FERNHURST
BOOKS

Copyright © 2015 Fernhurst Books Limited

This second edition first published in 2015 by Fernhurst Books Limited
62 Brandon Parade, Holly Walk, Leamington Spa, Warwickshire, CV32 4JE, UK
Tel: +44 (0) 1926 337488 | www.fernhurstbooks.com

All rights reserved. No part of this publication may be reproduced, stored in a retrieval system or transmitted, in any form or by any means, electronic, mechanical, photocopying, recording, scanning or otherwise, except under the terms of the Copyright, Designs and Patents Act 1988 or under the terms of a license issued by The Copyright Licensing Agency Ltd, Saffron House, 6-10 Kirby Street, London EC1N 8TS, UK, without the permission in writing of the Publisher.

Designations used by companies to distinguish their products are often claimed as trademarks. All brand names and product names used in this book are trade names, service marks, trademarks or registered trademarks of their respective owners. The Publisher is not associated with any product or vendor mentioned in this book.

This publication is designed to provide accurate and authoritative information in regard to the subject matter covered. It is sold on the understanding that the Publisher is not engaged in rendering professional services. If professional advice or other expert assistance is required, the services of a competent professional should be sought. The Publisher accepts no responsibilty for any errors or omissions, or for any accidents or mishaps which may arise from the use of this publication.

A catalogue record for this book is available from the British Library
ISBN 978-1-909911-26-0

Cover photograph by Tim Hore
Photographs on pages 1-10; 14-15; 17-22; 27-29; 31; 36; 38 (bottom); 40 by Tim Hore
Photographs on pages 11-13; 16; 24-26; 38 (top); 43; back cover © Rachel Atkins

Fernhurst Books and the authors would like to thank those who sailed fantastically on the photoshoots – Milo Gill-Taylor at Spinnaker Sailing Club and Katie Byne at Draycote Water Sailing Club, and their parents who accompanied them during the photoshoots.

Edited, designed & illustrated by Rachel Atkins
Printed in China through World Print

Contents

Foreword 4

Chapter 1   **Parts of the boat** 5

Chapter 2   **Rigging** 7

Chapter 3   **Your first sail** 11

Chapter 4   **Launching** 15

Chapter 5   **Reaching** 18

Chapter 6   **Beating** 21

Chapter 7   **Running** 24

Chapter 8   **Sailing a circular course** 27

Chapter 9   **Landing** 28

Chapter 10   **Safety** 31

Chapter 11   **How the wind moves your boat** 34

Chapter 12   **Knots** 36

Chapter 13   **The rules** 39

Chapter 14   **How to go faster** 40

Chapter 15   **What's next?** 45

Foreword

Sailing for Kids provides an introduction to sailing for children based on the Optimist dinghy. What is an Optimist? You will see from the photos that it is a single-handed boat for children, both boys and girls, up to the age of 15 and it is one of the most popular dinghies. It is sailed in countries around the world, in local flotillas and sailing clubs.

It is a great boat in which to learn to sail but it is also the boat many top class sailors have started in. As boys and girls become more skilful, many will learn to race in local regattas. For those that become very good, there is even a World Championship each year.

As the Optimist is so popular, it is easy to buy a second-hand one for a good price and it will keep its value.

Whether you start sailing in an Optimist or another type of dinghy, sailing is a great sport for children. It not only teaches them a new skill but it also fosters independence, self-respect, resilience, communication and organisation skills. Most importantly it is fun and many friendships that are made in Optimists are friends for life.

The Optimist Class Association in the UK is delighted to recommend this book. *Sailing for Kids* is a great introduction to our sport and whether you end up sailing for fun, club racing or aspire to reach Olympic standard, this book is an excellent starting point.

As a class association, we actively support local Optimist flotillas up and down the country encouraging local training and regattas and supporting parents and sailors at all points on their Optimist journey. Please check out our website: www.optimistsailing.org.uk. We are also affiliated with the International Optimist Dinghy Association (www.optiworld.org).

Enjoy your sailing.

Mark Lyttle
Chairman of the UK Optimist Class Association

1. Parts of the boat

The photo below and the one on the next page show an Optimist dinghy. The main parts of the boat are labelled. Try to remember as many as you can! These terms will be used in the book – if you can't remember what they mean, look back at these photos to remind yourself.

Roach
Curved edge of the sail (supported by battens)

Peak
Top of the sail

Head
Top edge of the sail

Burgee
Small flag that shows the direction of the wind

Leech
Back edge of the sail

Throat
Part of the sail at the top of the mast

Batten
Stiffening strip which supports the edge of the sail

Mast
Upright pole that the sail is attached to

Batten pocket
Pocket in the sail that the batten slides into

Sprit
Diagonal pole that holds the sail up

Clew
Back corner of the sail

Sprit adjuster
Rope used to adjust the position of the sprit

Outhaul
Rope to attach the corner of the sail to the end of the boom

Luff
Front edge of the sail

Sail tie
Used to tie the sail to the mast

Boom
Pole attached to the bottom edge of the sail

Foot
Bottom edge of the sail

Tack
Front corner of the sail

Boom jaw
Fitting which clips the boom onto the mast

Cringle
Hole in the sail to thread sail ties

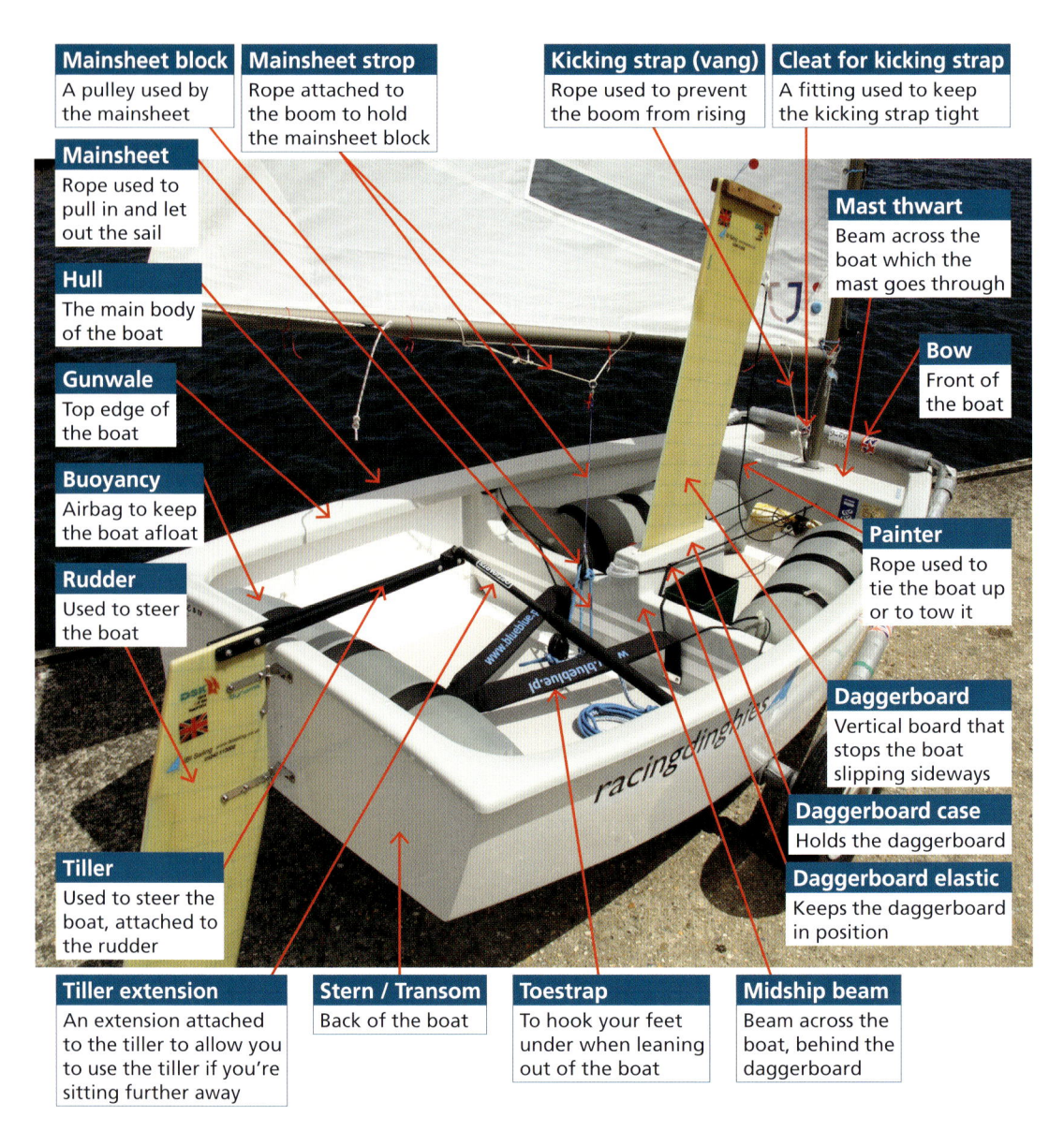

Chapter 1 Parts of the boat

Mainsheet block
A pulley used by the mainsheet

Mainsheet strop
Rope attached to the boom to hold the mainsheet block

Kicking strap (vang)
Rope used to prevent the boom from rising

Cleat for kicking strap
A fitting used to keep the kicking strap tight

Mainsheet
Rope used to pull in and let out the sail

Mast thwart
Beam across the boat which the mast goes through

Hull
The main body of the boat

Bow
Front of the boat

Gunwale
Top edge of the boat

Buoyancy
Airbag to keep the boat afloat

Painter
Rope used to tie the boat up or to tow it

Rudder
Used to steer the boat

Daggerboard
Vertical board that stops the boat slipping sideways

Daggerboard case
Holds the daggerboard

Tiller
Used to steer the boat, attached to the rudder

Daggerboard elastic
Keeps the daggerboard in position

Tiller extension
An extension attached to the tiller to allow you to use the tiller if you're sitting further away

Stern / Transom
Back of the boat

Toestrap
To hook your feet under when leaning out of the boat

Midship beam
Beam across the boat, behind the daggerboard

You can test how well you can remember the parts of the boat (and what they do) by printing off the photos with the labels missing:

- Fill in all the parts and descriptions you can remember.
- Check to see if you are correct.
- Go over the parts that you couldn't remember!

The photos (with labels missing) can be downloaded from:
www.fernhurstbooks.com/other-resources/sailing-for-kids

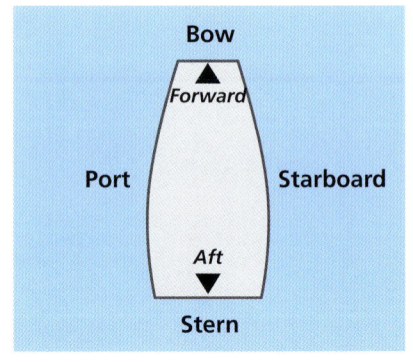

2. Rigging

Now you know what all the parts of the boat are, you are ready to put them together!

Rigging Setting up the sail and poles on your boat, ready to sail.

Lay the sail out on the floor (starboard side up), with the **boom** at the bottom.

Tie the sail onto the **boom** using the **sail ties** (threading them through the **cringles** on the sail and round the **boom**).

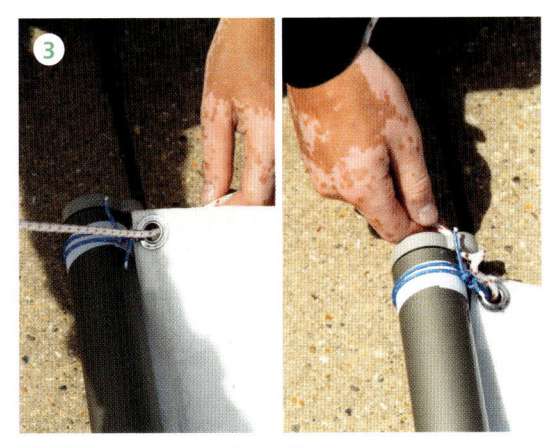

Tie the **outhaul** to the sail.

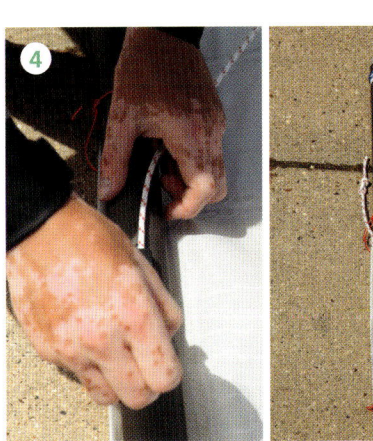

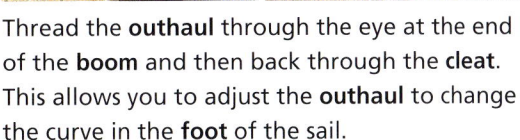

Thread the **outhaul** through the eye at the end of the **boom** and then back through the **cleat**. This allows you to adjust the **outhaul** to change the curve in the **foot** of the sail.

Chapter 2 Rigging

5 Thread the **sail ties** round the **mast**.

6 Move the **mast** up the sail, threading it through the **sail tie**s as you go.

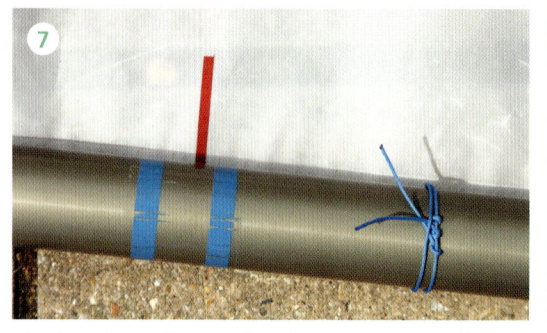

7 The band on the sail should be between the two markers on the **mast**.

8 Clip the **boom** onto the **mast**.

9 Hook the **sprit adjuster** onto the **mast**.

10 Attach the **peak** to the top of the **sprit**.

11 Loop the **sprit adjuster** to the bottom of the **sprit**.

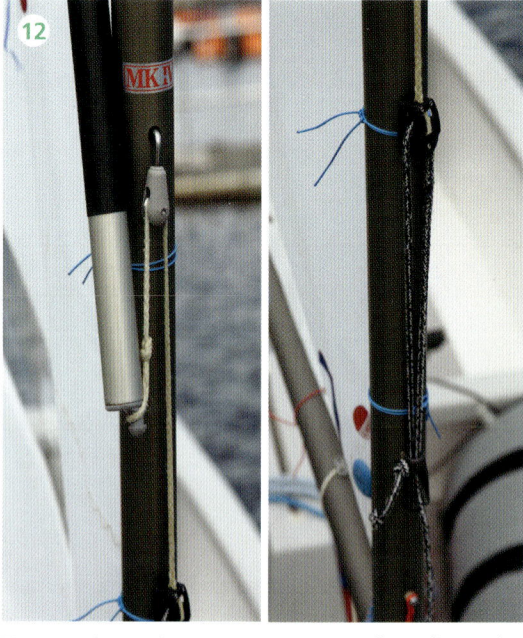

12 Ensure the **sprit arrangement** can be adjusted easily during sailing.

8

Chapter 2 **Rigging**

Tie the **throat** of the sail to the **mast**.

Thread the **burgee** into the two loops inside the **mast**.

Tie the **boom** to the **mast** to stop the boom being pulled down by the **kicking strap**.

Thread the **kicking strap** from the **boom** to the **cleat** on the **mast**.

Your sail is now ready for hoisting.

Chapter 2 Rigging

18 19

Put the **mast** through the hole in the **mast thwart**.  Ensure it is in the mast step on the **hull**.

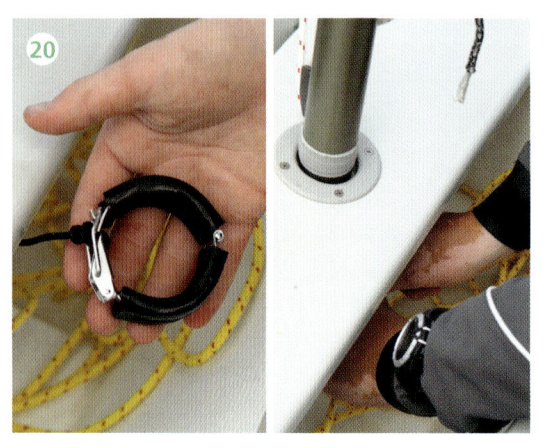

20 21

Attach the mast securing clamp to the **mast** under the **mast thwart**.

Check that the **mast** is in place and secure.

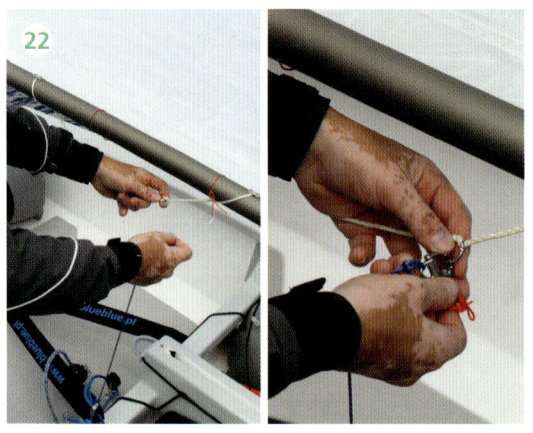

22 23

Attach the **mainsheet block** to the **mainsheet strop** using a clip.

Thread the **mainsheet** through the pulleys on the **hull**.

10

3. Your first sail

For your first sail, choose a warm day with a light wind.

What do I wear?

Wetsuit
If it is cold, or you are sailing on the sea, wear a wetsuit.

Spray Top
On top, wear a spray top to keep the wind out. Socks and sailing shoes will keep your feet warm.

Buoyancy Aid
Always wear a well-fitting buoyancy aid or lifejacket.

If you don't have a wetsuit or spray top, wear warm clothes, old trainers and a waterproof. *Do not* wear wellington boots because they may fill with water! Whatever you are wearing, **always** wear a well-fitting buoyancy aid or lifejacket.

Chapter 3 Your first sail

Where do I sit?

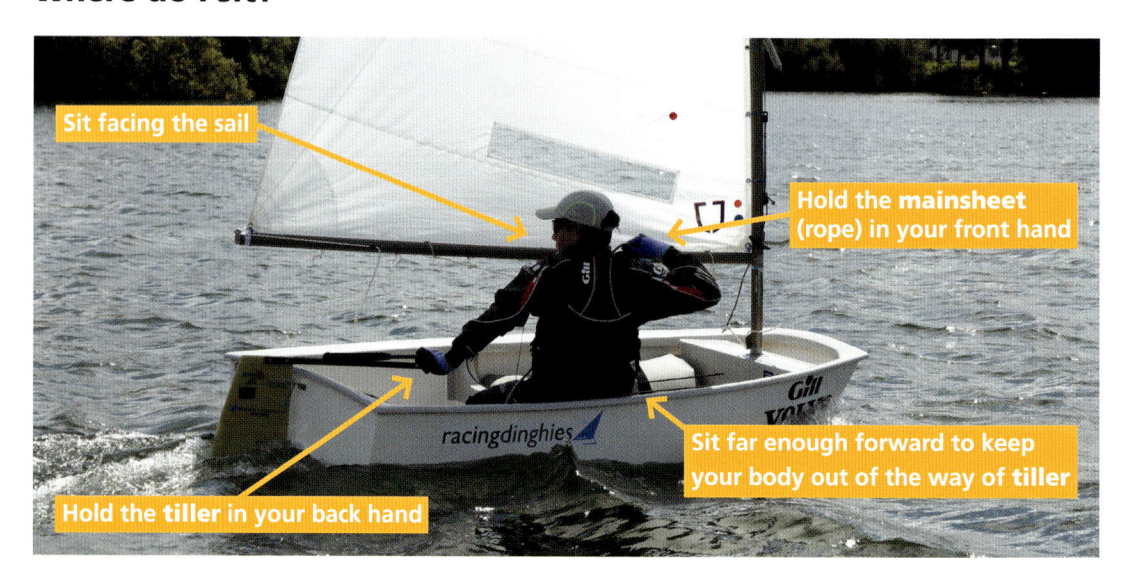

- Sit facing the sail
- Hold the **mainsheet** (rope) in your front hand
- Sit far enough forward to keep your body out of the way of **tiller**
- Hold the **tiller** in your back hand

How do I steer?
To steer the boat you move the **tiller**.

Pull tiller towards you
Pull the tiller towards your body to steer the boat away from you.

Keep tiller central
Hold the tiller in the middle of the boat to steer straight ahead.

Push tiller away from you
Push the tiller away from your body to steer the boat towards you.

Chapter 3 Your first sail

How do I speed up, slow down and stop?
To change the boat's speed you need to move the sail. You use the **mainsheet** to do this.

Speeding up
To make the boat go faster, pull in the mainsheet to pull in the sail. This is also known as *sheeting in*.

Slowing down and stopping
To slow the boat down, let out the mainsheet to let out the sail. This is also know as *sheeting out*. To stop completely, let go of the mainsheet.

What if I stop by mistake?
Sometimes you can stop by mistake because your boat is pointing into the wind. This is known as being *in irons*. If this happens you need to change the direction of the boat to get going again.

Push out the **boom** and the **tiller**.

This will make the boat go backwards and turn away from the wind.

When the boat is sideways to the wind, stop pushing the **boom**. *Sheet in* and straighten the **tiller** to get going.

13

Chapter 3 Your first sail

Your first sail

Now that you know the basics, you are ready for your first sail. Start off with:
- The **wind** blowing towards the side of the boat.
- The **mainsheet** pulled halfway in.
- The **tiller** central.
- The **daggerboard** fully down (to stop the boat from drifting sideways).

1
Sail with the wind blowing towards the side of the boat. Continue like this until you want to turn round.

2
Push the **tiller** away from you to turn. As the boat turns the sail will swing towards you – duck under the **boom**!

3
Move to the other side of the boat (still being careful not to hit your head on the **boom**!).

4
Make sure you continue to look where you are heading while crossing the boat.

5
Swap hands so that the **tiller** is in your back hand and the **mainsheet** is in your front hand.

6
Once you are settled on the new side of the boat, centre the **tiller** and sail back to where you started.

4. Launching

Launching Putting a boat in the water and sailing away from the shore.

Launching is done differently depending on where the wind is blowing from. It is easiest to launch a boat when the wind is blowing along the shore.

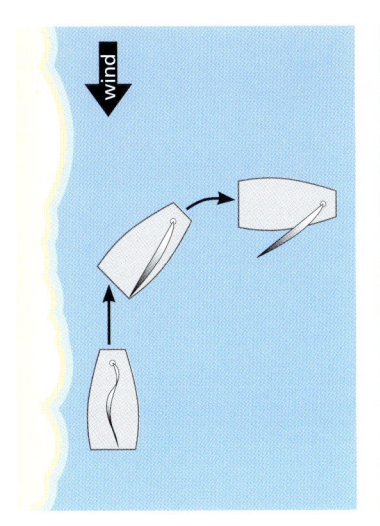

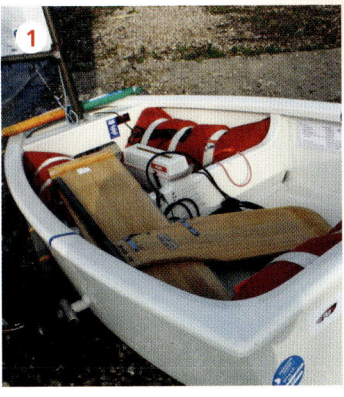

1 Lay the **daggerboard** and **rudder** in the bottom of the boat.

2 Tie the boat to the trolley and wheel them into the water.

3 Hold the boat or **painter** (rope) and push the boat off the trolley.

4 Hold the boat pointing into the wind (*head to wind*). Ask a friend to take the trolley.

5 Clip on the **rudder**.

Chapter 4 Launching

Swing the boat round and get in.

Push the **daggerboard** halfway into its case.

Pull in the sail and sail away.

Launching from a windward shore

If the wind is blowing from the shore to the water, you will be launching from a *windward shore*. You launch from a windward shore as you would if the wind is blowing along the shore (photos above), except this time the boat will be *head to wind* when it is pointing at the shore.

Take care, the wind will be stronger when you get away from the land. And if you get into trouble, the wind will blow you further away from the shore.

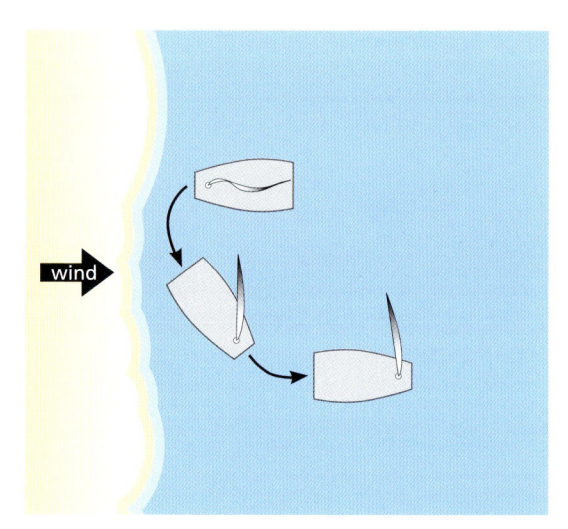

Launching from a leeward shore

If the wind is blowing from the water to the shore, you will be launching from a *leeward shore*. This is more difficult than launching from a windward shore, as this time you are trying to get your boat to go against the wind. However, it is safer because if you get into trouble, the wind will blow you back towards the shore. See the photos opposite.

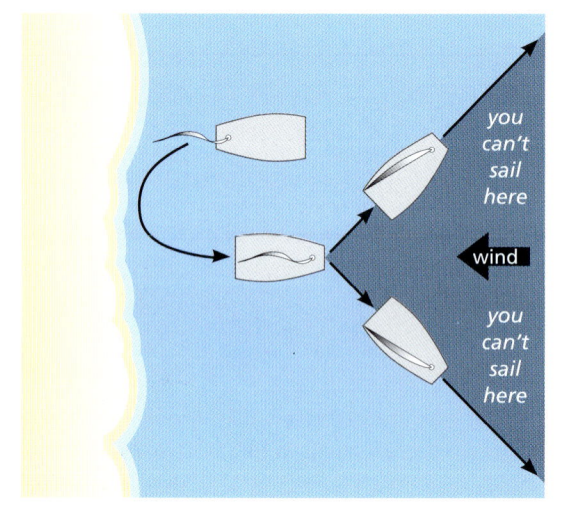

Chapter 4 Launching

1. Rig the boat, but unclip the **mainsheet** to let the sail turn round to flap in the wind.

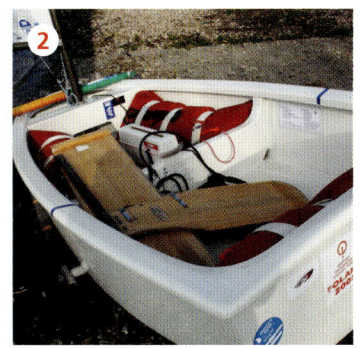

2. Lay the **daggerboard** and **rudder** in the bottom of the boat.

3. Tie the boat to the trolley and wheel them into the water.

4. Push the boat off the trolley. Ask a friend to take the trolley.

5. Turn the boat to point into the wind. Clip on the **mainsheet**.

6. Push the boat into deeper water. Clip on the **rudder** and slot in the **daggerboard**.

7. Point the boat in the direction in which you will sail (not directly into the wind). Push off and get in.

8. Quickly push the **daggerboard** down to stop you going sideways (but not so far down that it hits the ground).

9. Pull in the **mainsheet**. Sail off, as close to the wind as you can.

17

5. Reaching

Reaching Sailing across the wind, with the wind blowing towards the side of your boat.

Reaching is fun, fast and easy to control.

How do I know where the wind is coming from?
You can tell the direction of the wind by looking at your **burgee**. (You can also look out for ripples in the water.) If you unclip your **mainsheet**, the sail will blow away from the wind. For reaching, your boat should be side on to the wind.

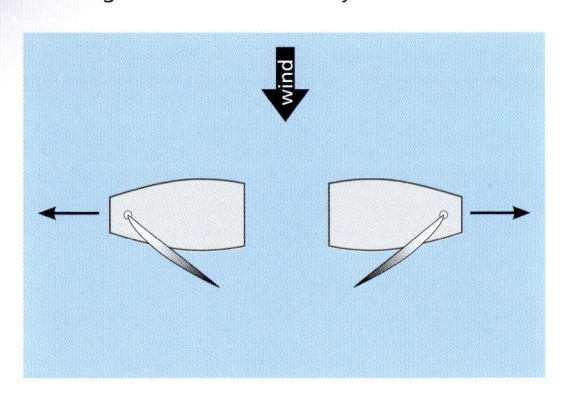

Where do I sit when reaching?
The wind will be blowing towards the side of your boat, so sit on the side with the wind coming from behind you.

Normal wind
Sit in the boat, just behind the **midship beam**.

Strong wind
If the wind is strong sit on the **gunwale**, to balance the boat.

Chapter 5 Reaching

Practise reaching
Start off with:
- The **wind** blowing towards the side of your boat.
- The **mainsheet** pulled halfway in.
- The **tiller** central. (Hold the tiller gently, and make only small movements, otherwise the boat will turn too quickly.)
- The **daggerboard** fully down. (As you become more confident when reaching you can sail with the daggerboard halfway up – this will help you to go faster.)

Controlling your speed by adjusting the sail
Don't forget that you can control your speed with the **mainsheet**. To adjust the **mainsheet** for maximum speed, keep to a straight course (by keeping the **tiller** central).

Let out the sail by letting out the **mainsheet** until the **luff** (front edge of the sail) begins to flap or back. This will slow you down.

Pull in the sail until it stops flapping by pulling in the **mainsheet**. This will make you go faster. Keeping the sail adjusted like this will ensure you are always going at maximum speed.

Beware of gusts
You can tell if a gust is approaching because the water looks dark as a gust travels over it. When a gust hits the boat, lean back (*hike out*) to balance the boat. If the boat still tips over (*heels*), let the **mainsheet** out a bit. If a gust makes the boat turn, use the **tiller** to steer back to the direction that you wanted.

Chapter 5 Reaching

Different types of reaching
There are three types of reaching, depending on the angle of your boat in relation to the wind:

Beam reaching Reaching when your boat is completely side on to the wind.
Close reaching Reaching when your boat is angled slightly towards the wind.
Broad reaching Reaching when your boat is angled slightly away from the wind.

Beam reaching
To remain completely side on to the wind, keep the **tiller** central.

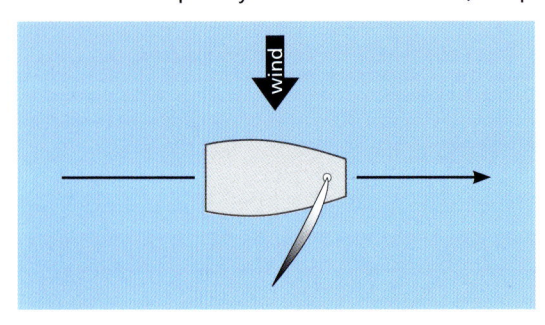

Close reaching
To sail closer to the wind, push the **tiller** away from you and then straighten up. (You will have to pull the **mainsheet** in a little to stop the sail flapping.)

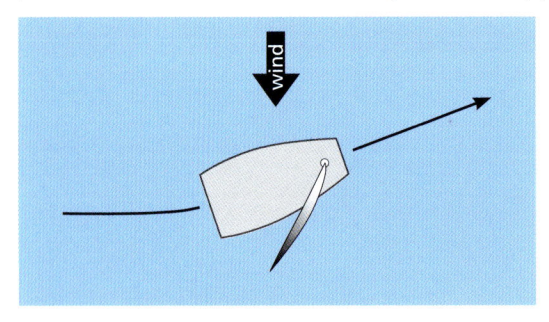

Broad reaching
To sail slightly away from the wind, pull the **tiller** towards you and then straighten up. (You can let out the sail quite a lot before the front edge flaps.)

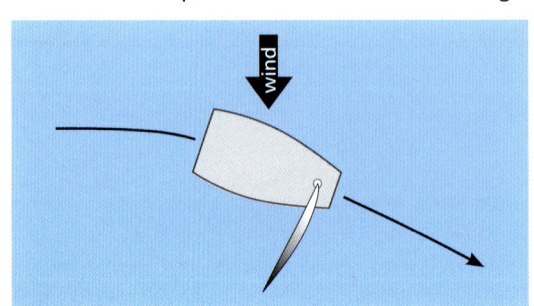

6. Beating

Beating Sailing a zigzag course towards the wind.
Tacking Changing direction *through the wind* while sailing towards the wind. (The **boom** crosses the boat as the wind goes from one side of the boat to the other.)

You can't sail straight into the wind. If you try to, the boat just stops (being *in irons*, see page 9). The only way to sail towards the wind is to follow a zigzag course (so you are never sailing directly into the wind). This is **beating**. Changing direction between each leg of the zigzag is **tacking**.

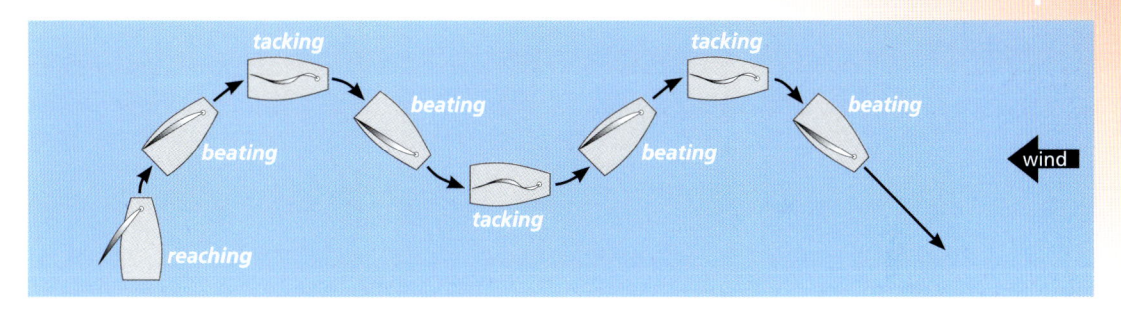

Where do I sit when beating?

Sit in the boat so that your front leg touches the **midship beam**.

Do **not** sit too far forward (because the **bow** will dig in to the water), or too far back (because the **stern** will drag through the water).

Chapter 6 Beating

Use your weight to balance the boat in windy weather.

Windy weather
As the wind picks up, sit on the **gunwale** to balance the boat.

Extremely windy weather
If the wind gets even stronger, think about leaning out (*hiking*) to balance the stronger force of the wind.

Practise beating

1 Begin on a *reach*, with the **daggerboard** fully down.

2 Pull in the **mainsheet** until the **boom** is over the back (*aft*) corner of the boat.

3 Push the **tiller** away to turn slowly towards the wind. Watch the **luff** (front edge of the sail).

4 When the **luff** begins to flap or back, pull the **tiller** towards you to turn away from the wind a little.

5 Centre the **tiller** to straighten up. You are now sailing as close to the wind as you can.

6 Continue sailing in this direction to complete one leg of the beat. Before you start the new leg (zigzag) you need to *tack* (see next page).

Chapter 6 **Beating**

Tacking
Tacking is a vital part of beating – it lets you to go from one zigzag leg of the beat to the next.

1 Pick up some speed before you begin to tack.

2 Push the **tiller** away from you to begin the turn (and keep it pushed out throughout the turn).

3 The sail will flap and the **boom** will swing towards you – duck under the **boom**!

4 As the **boom** and sail swing towards you, move across to the other side of the boat.

5 As you cross the boat, keep holding onto the **mainsheet** with your front hand, and hold the **tiller** behind your back. Keep facing forwards.

6 Once on the other side of the boat, bring your **mainsheet** hand behind your back to hold both the **mainsheet** and the **tiller**.

7 With the **mainsheet** and **tiller** now in your back hand, bring your front hand forward.

8 Take the **mainsheet** with your front hand, and pull it in. Tack complete! (Now sail the next leg of your beat, and then tack again.)

23

7. Running

Running Sailing away from the wind (like being blown across the water!).
Gybing Changing direction on a run so the wind comes from the other side of the boat. (The **boom** crosses the boat as the wind goes from one side to the other.)

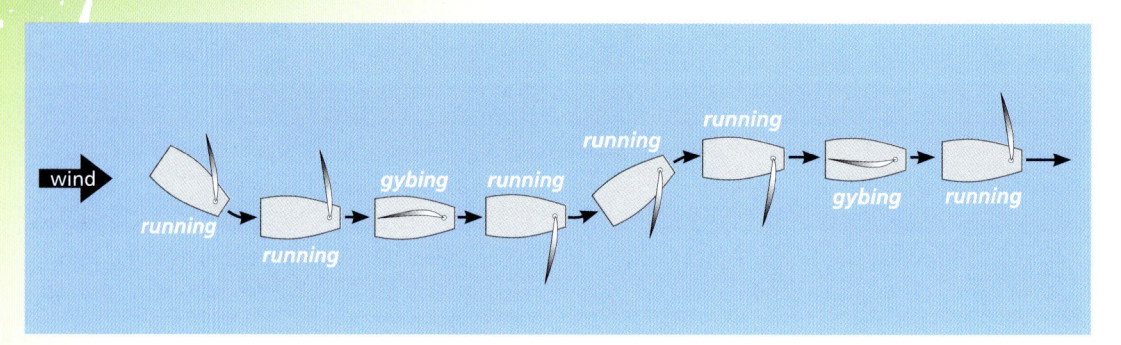

Where do I sit when running?
To begin with, sit in the middle of the boat.

24

Chapter 7 **Running**

Practise running

1

Begin on a *reach*. (When you start practising *running* the **daggerboard** should be fully down, but as you become more confident you can sail with the **daggerboard** halfway or fully up – this will help you to go faster.)

2

Pull the **tiller** towards you slightly to turn away from the wind. *(Be careful not to pull the **tiller** too much, as this would cause the wind to blow into the sail from the other side, and you would begin to gybe.)*

3

Once you have turned away from the wind, centre the **tiller** to straighten up.

4

Let out the **mainsheet** until the **boom** is out (at a right angle to the boat). Continue sailing like this until you want to change direction. You will then need to *gybe* (see next page).

Chapter 7 **Running**

Gybing

Just as tacking is a vital part of beating, gybing is a vital part of running. This time, you are changing direction while sailing away from the wind.

1. Make sure you are on a *run* (the wind blowing from behind the boat).

2. If the **daggerboard** is fully up, push it halfway down.

3. Grab all the parts of the **mainsheet** with your front hand.

4. Begin the turn by pulling the **tiller** and **mainsheet** towards you.

5. Duck under the **boom** as the sail moves across the boat.

6. Move across to the other side of the boat, keeping the **mainsheet** in your front hand and the **tiller** in your back hand.

7. Once on the other side, swap hands on the **mainsheet** and the **tiller**.

8. Continue to sail on a *run* in your new direction.

26

8. Sailing a circular course

You have learnt about the three different points of sailing – **reaching**, **beating** and **running**, plus changing direction *through the wind* – **tacking** and **gybing**. Now you are ready to put them all together! Sailing in a circle allows you to practise each point of sailing.

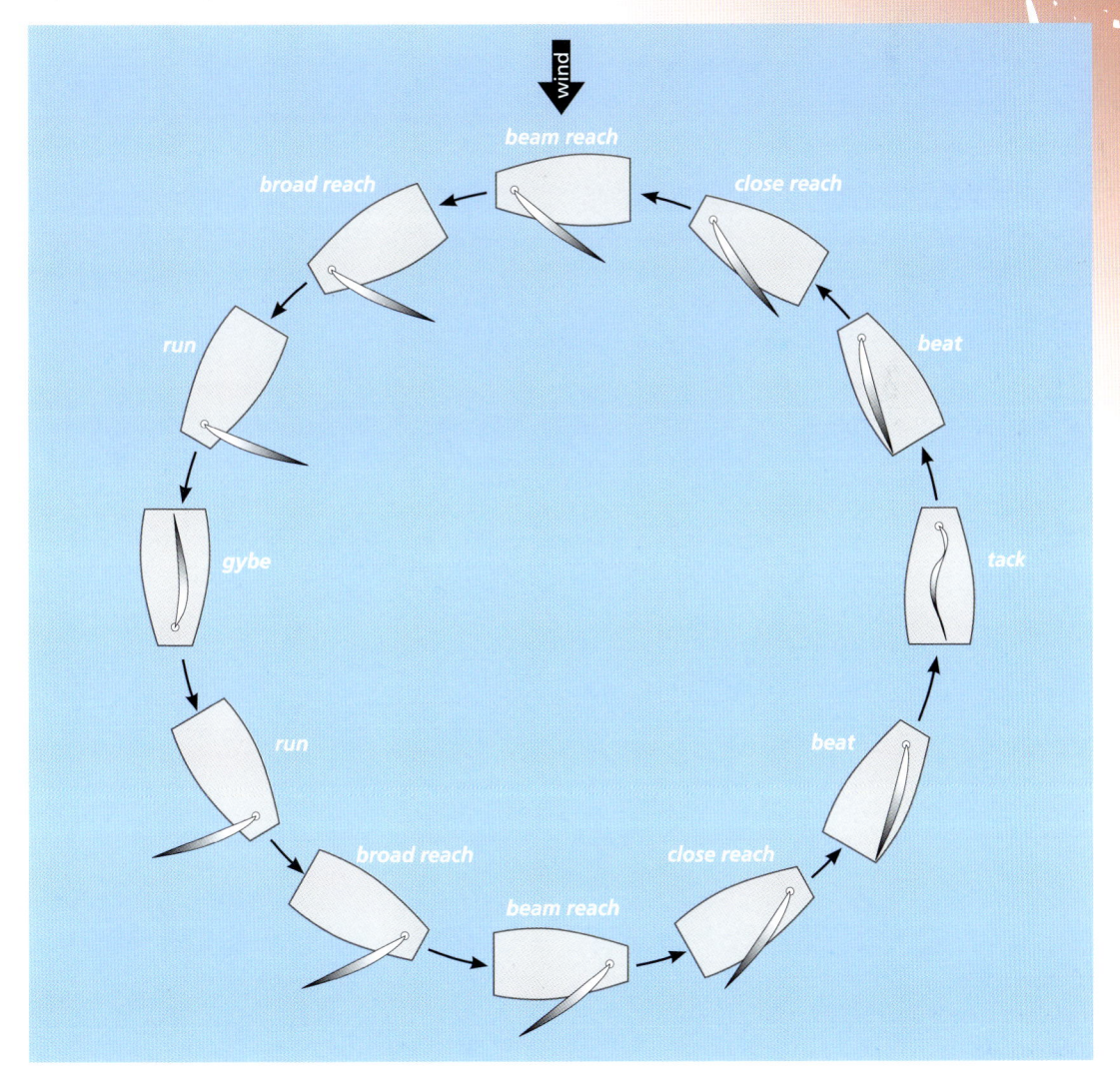

9. Landing

Landing Sailing into the shore and getting out of the boat.

As with launching (page 11), how you land depends on the wind direction. It is easiest to land a boat when the wind is blowing along the shore.

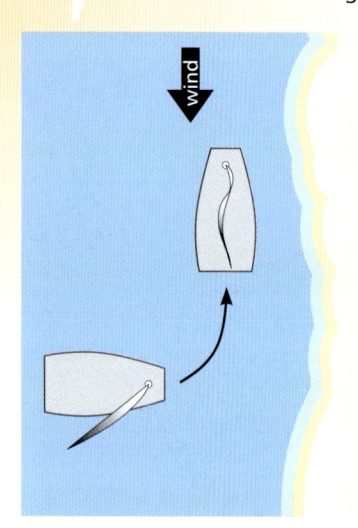

1 Sail towards the shore on a *reach*.

2 Let the **mainsheet** out a bit (to slow down) and lift the **daggerboard** up to halfway.

3 Turn into the wind (to stop) and take the **daggerboard** out completely.

4 Jump out of the boat.

5 Take the **rudder** off.

Chapter 9 **Landing**

Ask a friend to bring the trolley.

Float the boat onto the trolley.

Pull the trolley and boat ashore.

Landing on a windward shore
If the wind is blowing from the shore to the water, you will be landing on a *windward shore*. You land on a windward shore as you would if the wind is blowing along the shore (photos above), except:
- You sail towards the shore on a *beat* (rather than a *reach*).
- When you steer to face the wind you will be pointing at the shore (rather than being side on to the shore).

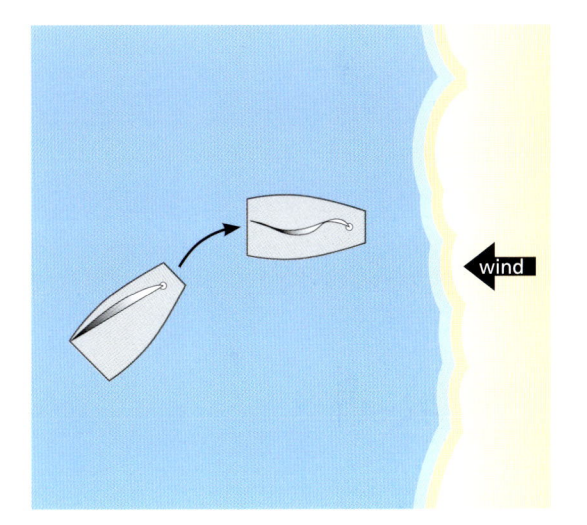

Landing on a leeward shore
If the wind is blowing from the water to the shore, you will be landing on a *leeward shore*. To do this you need to slow down slightly differently. See the photos on the next page.

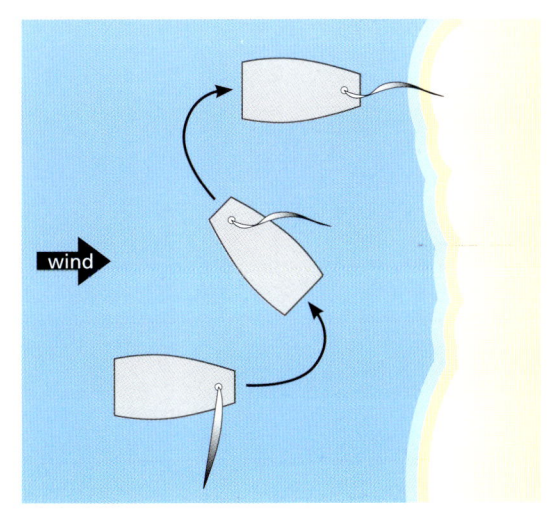

29

Chapter 9 **Landing**

1 Sail towards the shore on a *run*.	 **2** When near the shore, turn into the wind and unclip the **mainsheet**.	 **3** Turn back towards the shore (your sail will point to the shore).
 **4** Pull out the **daggerboard**.	 **5** Jump out of the boat.	 **6** Unclip the **rudder**.
 **7** Ask a friend to bring the trolley.	 **8** Float the boat onto the trolley.	 **9** Pull the trolley and boat ashore.

10. Safety

Personal safety
- Before you even think about sailing, make sure you are able to swim 25 metres and float for 30 seconds.
- Always wear a **buoyancy aid** or **lifejacket** when you are near or on the water. Look after it – it could save your life one day! Make sure it is an approved type and fits you properly. When you're wearing it, make sure it is fastened correctly and fully inflated.
- If you have long hair, tie it back or wear a hat (otherwise it could get caught on parts of the boat).
- Always tell someone when you are going out sailing. Never sail without telling someone first!
- If you start to feel cold while sailing, go ashore and get warmed up!

Equipment
- Check the boat's **buoyancy** each time you go out sailing. Don't sail if the buoyancy airbags are punctured or not fully inflated.
- Make sure you use the **mast securing clamp** to attach the **mast** to the boat, so that the rig doesn't fall out if the boat turns upside down.
- Make sure you use a **clip** to attach the **mainsheet pulley** to the **mainsheet strop**, so that you can easily free the sail when launching and landing.
- If the wind gets too strong while sailing, take off the **sprit** to reduce the sail.
- Always take a **bucket** with you so that you can bail out if your boat fills with water. Tie the bucket to the toestraps so you don't lose it if you capsize! (A small bailer and a sponge are also useful.)
- Always take a **paddle** with you so that you can get back to shore if the wind drops.

Sailing without the sprit in heavy wind.

Using buckets to bail out.

Chapter 10 Safety

Getting help
- If you need help, use the International Distress Signal:

Wave you arms up.	Move them out to the side.	Then move them down.

- Along with arm waving, you can also blow a **whistle** to help draw attention. The Optimist Class require you to have a whistle when sailing.

Capsizing
- If you capsize, always stay with the boat. Never try to swim to shore – it's further than it looks!
- To recover from a capzise:

You're about to go...    ... and you're in!

Always stay with the boat.    Pull the **daggerboard** fully down (if not already).

Chapter 10 Safety

5 Grab the **daggerboard** with both hands and pull it down towards you to turn the boat upright. Putting your feet on the underside of the boat will help.

6 As the boat turns to its side, allow the boat to point towards the wind. Change your grip on the **daggerboard** so that you can push it into the water.

7 Continue to push the **daggerboard** until you can no longer reach it, then use your feet to push it further into the water.

8 Grab the side of the boat and make sure it is completely upright.

9 Grip the **gunwale** and pull yourself into the boat.

10 Now use a bucket and/or bailer to *bail out*. Once the water is out of your boat, either continue with your sail, sail ashore or signal for help if you need it.

33

11. How the wind moves your boat

The wind hitting your sail makes your boat move forward when sailing. As you move through the different points of sailing – **running, reaching** and **beating** – the direction from which the wind blows towards your boat changes. So the way the wind moves your boat forward changes too.

Running

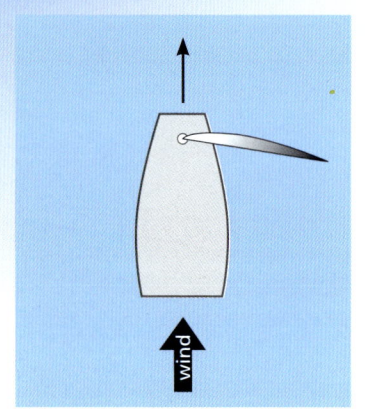

Reaching & Beating

When you are *running*, the wind is blowing from behind and causes your boat to move forward.

The sail fills with air and swings out to the side. Your boat is pushed along in the direction of the wind, just like a feather on the water.

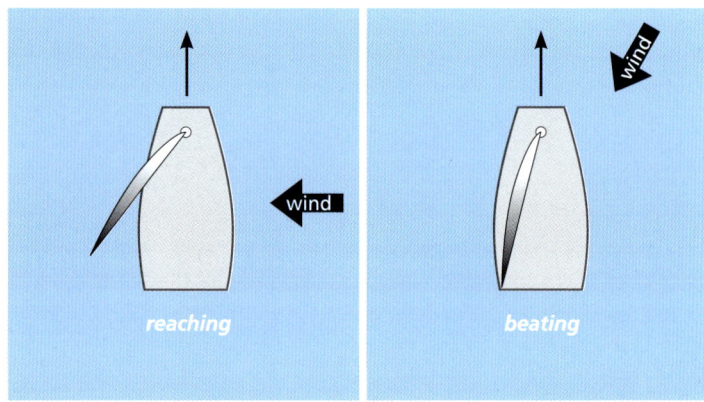

When you are *reaching* or *beating*, the wind is blowing towards you from the side, but still causes your boat to move forward.

The boat is actually 'squeezed' forward (rather than being pushed sideways in the direction of the wind). Imagine you are holding a slippery bar of soap between your thumb and your finger. If you squeeze your thumb and finger together, the bar of soap will shoot forwards. Now, imagine that the bar of soap is your boat, your thumb is the wind, and your finger is the **daggerboard**. When the **daggerboard** is fully down it resists the force of the wind, and the boat moves forward (just like the bar of slippery soap shooting through the air!).

With the wind hitting your sail from the side, your boat may feel like it is going to tip over (*heel*). Sitting on the *windward side* (closest to the wind) of the boat means that your body weight counteracts the force of the wind, keeping your boat upright.

Chapter 11 **How the wind moves your boat**

Adjusting the daggerboard

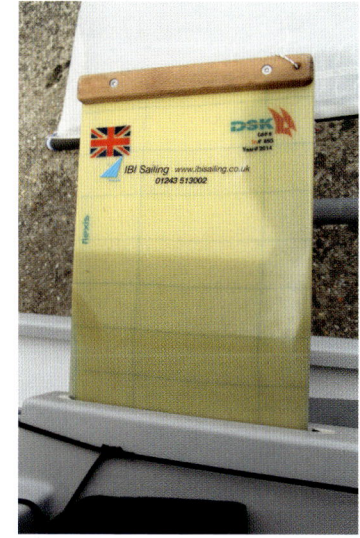

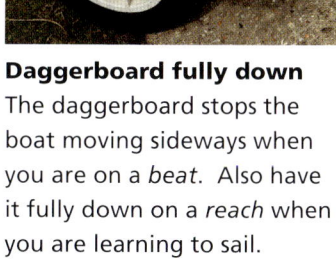

Daggerboard fully down
The daggerboard stops the boat moving sideways when you are on a *beat*. Also have it fully down on a *reach* when you are learning to sail.

Daggerboard halfway up
When you become more confident sailing on a *reach* you can lift the daggerboard halfway up. This will make you go faster. Also have it halfway up on a *run* when you are learning to sail.

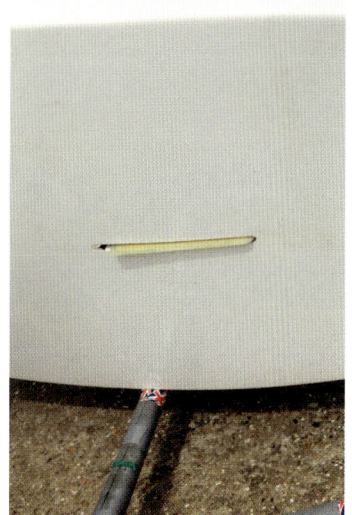

Daggerboard fully up
When the daggerboard is fully up there is no daggerboard left in the water. This is great when you are on a *run*, being pushed forward by the wind. It does mean that you will go faster, but it also makes the boat more tippy, so only have the daggerboard fully up when you are very confident.

35

12. Knots

Knot A fastening or tie made with ropes or string.

There are lots of knots, each with a different job. Here are the most common knots, which are all very useful for sailing. Try them out a couple of times, and then see if you can do them without looking at the instructions!

Bowline
Use to make a secure loop in a rope that will not slip (e.g. attaching the **kicking strap** to the **boom**).

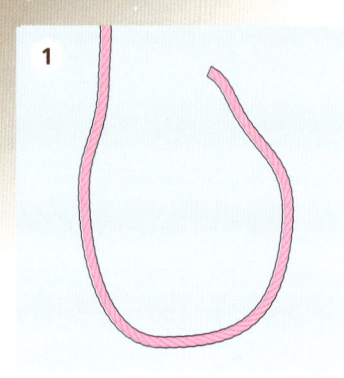

1 Form a bight (open loop) of the required size.

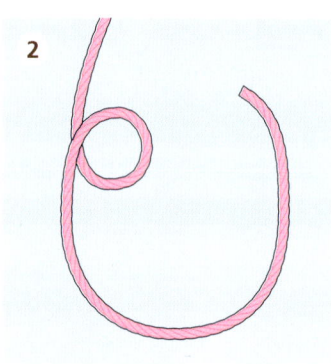

2 Make a small loop.

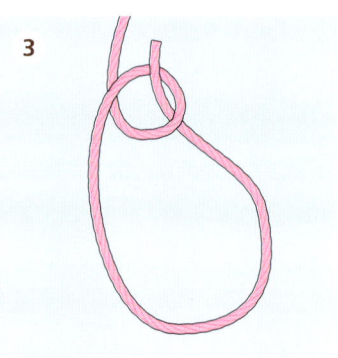

3 Pass the end of the rope up through the small loop.

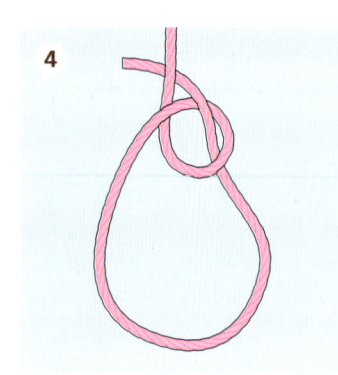

4 Then pass it behind the part of the rope that's hanging.

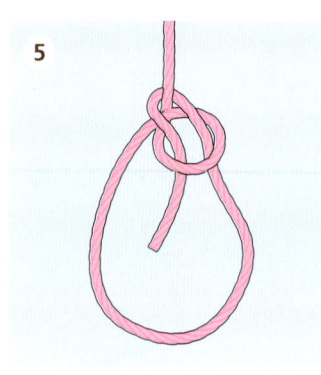

5 Then pass it down through the small loop.

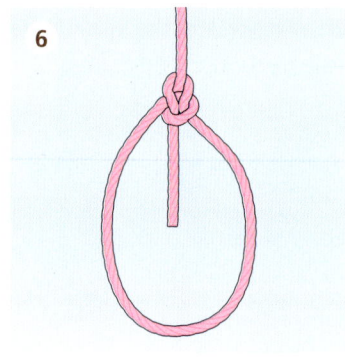

6 Pull the end of the rope tight, and check there is a long tail.

Chapter 12 **Knots**

Round turn & two half hitches
Use to attach a rope to a pole or ring (e.g. attaching the **painter** to a mooring ring).

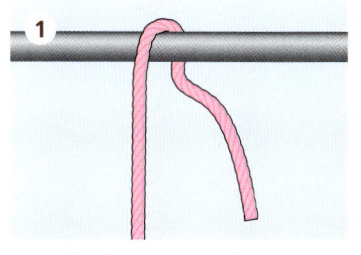

1. Pass the loose end of the rope over the pole. 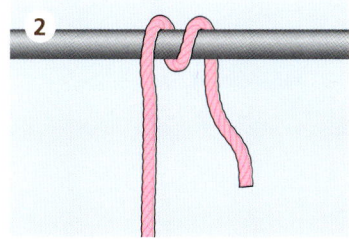
2. Then take another complete turn around the pole. 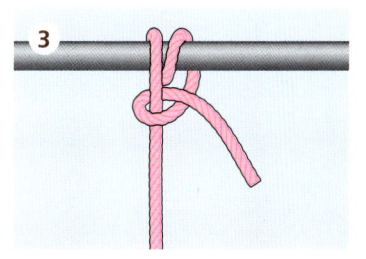
3. Take the loose end over the standing part, around it and back through to form a half hitch. 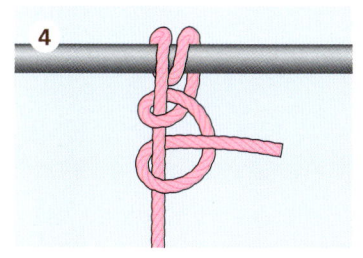
4. Repeat, to form a second half hitch. 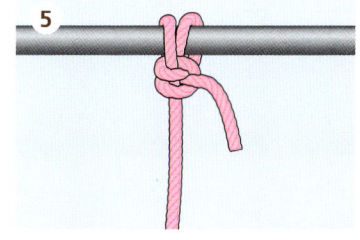
5. Pull tight.

Figure of eight
Use to stop the end of a rope being pulled through a hole (e.g. on the end of the **mainsheet**).

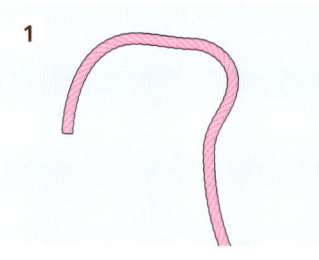

1. Make a bight (open loop). 
2. Make a loop. 
3. Pass the loose end of the rope under the rest of the rope to form a figure 8. 
4. Pass the loose end of the rope through the top loop.
5. Pull tight.

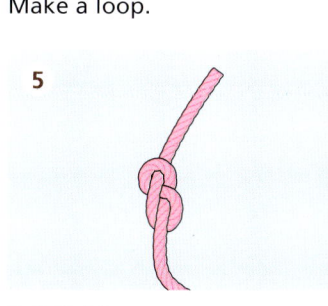

Chapter 12 Knots

Reef knot

Use to tie two ends of rope together (e.g. for securing **sail ties**).

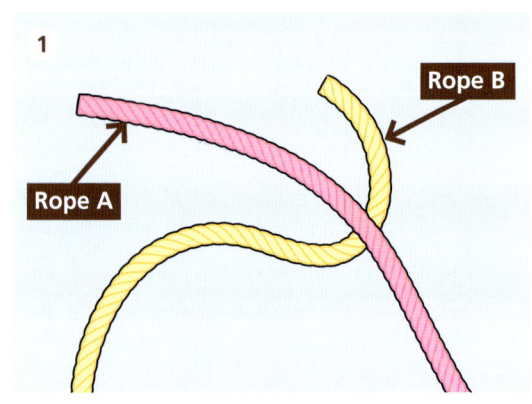

1

Rope B

Rope A

Begin with two ropes. Pass the loose end of rope A over rope B.

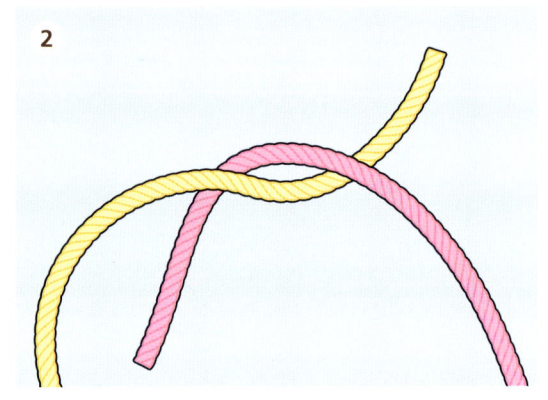

2

Pass the loose end of rope A down, underneath rope B.

3

Bring the loose end of rope A back up over rope B.

4

Pass the loose end of rope B under the loose end of rope A.

5

Pass the loose end of rope B round over rope A, and then pass it through the left hand loop.

6

Pull the ropes tight, and then check you have done it correctly!

13. The rules

The rules help keep you safe while sailing. If there are a lot of boats on the water at one time, they may crash into each other. The rules tell you which boat is supposed to move where, to avoid a collision.

Here are the two most important rules to remember:

Windward boat gives way

Windward boat The boat nearer to the wind.
Leeward boat The boat further away from the wind.

If both boats are on the same tack (the wind is hitting their sails from the same side), then the windward boat must keep clear.

The red boat must keep clear of the green boat.

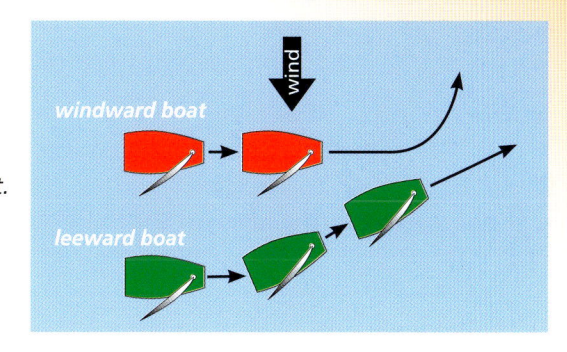

Port gives way to starboard

Port tack Sailing with the wind blowing towards the left (port) side of the boat.
Starboard tack Sailing with the wind blowing towards the right (starboard) side of the boat.

If one boat is on port tack and the other is on starboard tack, the boat on port tack must keep clear.

The red boat must keep clear of the green boat.

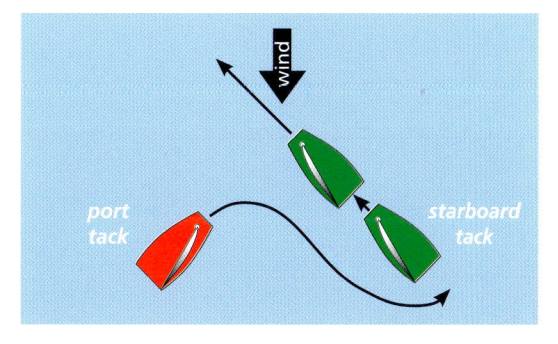

14. How to go faster

Now that you have learnt the basics, get practising until you become really confident on the water! Then you will be ready to learn how to go faster. This is when the fun really begins!

Going faster in different wind strengths
You need to adjust the rig to achieve maximum speed in different wind strengths. You will need to adjust:
- The **sail ties** around the mast.
- The **sprit adjuster**.
- The **kicking strap** (vang).
- The **outhaul**.
- The **mainsheet strop** position.

Strong winds
In strong winds you need everything to be very tight. It's best to set up the rig ashore with a friend helping you.
- The **sail ties** around the **mast** must be really tight, otherwise a gap will open between the sail and the mast. Pull each tie tight and tie half a **reef knot** (page 34). Ask a friend to put a finger on it to keep it tight while you finish the knot.
- The **kicking strap** (vang) and **sprit** work against each other, so you have to tighten them alternately, a little at a time. First pull on the kicking strap, then the sprit. Repeat, pulling them on one after the other until they are both tight.

1	2	3
The sprit is too loose.	Pull it tighter.	Now the sail sets without creases.

Chapter 14 How to go faster

- Start with the **outhaul** fairly tight. When you are sailing, you may find you can handle more power, in which case let off the outhaul a bit.
- Attach the **mainsheet block** towards the back (aft) end of the **strop**.

Light winds
In light winds, you want everything to be less tight.
- Adjust the **sail ties** until the sail just touches the **mast**.
- Tighten the **sprit adjuster**, then let it off until all the creases disappear.
- To set the **kicking strap** (vang), pull in the **mainsheet** as you would for beating. Then pull the kicking strap until it is just tight, and cleat it.
- Surprisingly, you need the **outhaul** to be quite tight in light winds.
- The **mainsheet** should be attached to the centre or front of the **strop**.

Setting the mast rake
- Attach a tape measure to the top of your **mast**. Ask a friend to pull the mast back. While your friend is doing this, measure from the top of the mast to the middle of the top of the **transom**.
- Ask your friend to move the mast until the distance from the mast to the transom is between 270 and 275cm. Your boat should now be well balanced (steer easily).
- If there is too much pull on the **tiller** when you're beating, rake (point) the mast forward (but rake the mast back if you need more 'feel').
- Ideally, the boat should turn slowly into the wind if you let go of the tiller. This is *weather helm*. If the boat turns away from the wind when you let go of the tiller, it is *lee helm*. You can stop this by raking the mast back.

Going faster when beating

Adjusting the rig
- Tighten the **sprit adjuster.**
- Put the **daggerboard** right down. Use the **daggerboard elastic** so that the daggerboard is raked back in the water.
- Let out the **mainsheet** until the **boom** is above the corner of the **transom**.

What you do
- Sit in the middle of the boat. If you sit too far back the **stern** will drag through the water, and if you sit too far forward the **bow** will dig in to the water (both of which will slow you down).
- Move your body sideways to keep the boat flat all of the time.
- Steer with the **tiller extension**. This lets you move about while still controlling the **rudder**.
- Hold the tiller extension across your body so you can use your tiller (back) hand to help adjust the **mainsheet**. (Never use your teeth to hold the mainsheet.)
- Watch the **luff** (front of the sail) and **telltales** (strips of wool or tape on each side of the sail) carefully.
- Keep turning towards the wind until the front of the sail begins to back or the windward

Chapter 14 How to go faster

telltale (on the side of the sail nearer the wind) starts pointing downwards and flapping. Then pull the **tiller** and turn slightly away from the wind until the sail fills and the telltales are both streaming along the sail together. You are now on course.
- Keep repeating this because the wind is always changing its direction.

Watch the **luff** and **telltales**.	The **telltales** should be streaming along the sail together.	If the **windward telltale** drops or points forward, or the **luff** backs, bear away slightly.	If the **leeward telltale** points forward, head up slightly.

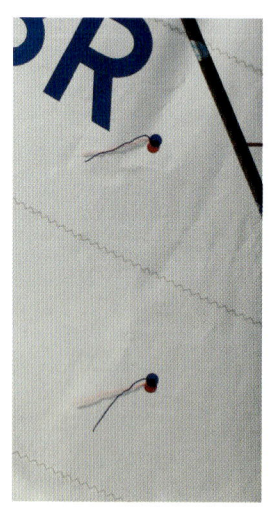

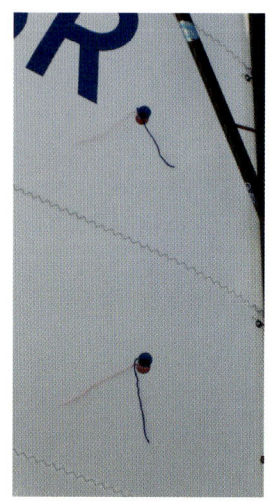

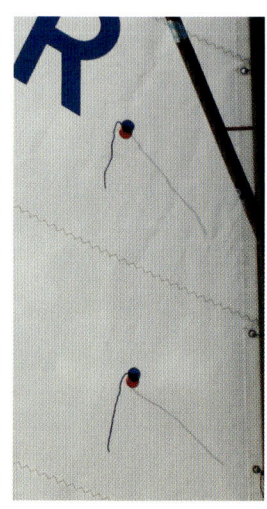

Beating in light winds

- Make sure you have a very sensitive **burgee** so that you can tell where the wind is coming from even when it is very light!
- The **sprit** should be looser than normal.
- Let out the **mainsheet** until the boat begins to move. (The **boom** may go out beyond the corner of the boat.)
- Sit in front of the **midship beam**, with your feet behind it. Lean against the **daggerboard case** and move sideways until the boat is level. Sit still, or you will shake the wind out of the sail.
- Don't tack too often as this slows you down.

Beating in strong winds

- Everything should be very tight.
- *Hike* hard: Put your feet under the nearest **toestrap** and lean back as far as you can, with the **gunwale** under your knees and your bottom over the side of the boat.
- If you cannot keep the boat upright, raise the **daggerboard** a little.

Chapter 14 How to go faster

- Sit just behind the **midship beam**. But if the **bow** starts to dig in to the water, move back.
- Use a ratchet block to help you hold the **mainsheet**. 'Clamp' the mainsheet between your hand and the **gunwale**. Only let out the mainsheet if the boat still heels (tips) when you are fully hiked.
- You may find a lot of water comes into the boat. *Bail* by holding the **tiller** and **mainsheet** in you back hand, with the bailer in your front hand. Scoop the water out of the boat over your front shoulder.

Going faster when reaching
As you bear away onto a reach (from a beat), a lot of things need doing:
- Pull up the **daggerboard** about halfway. A good guide is to raise the daggerboard until the **boom** just clears it.
- Hold the **mainsheet** in your tiller extension hand, then move forward and let off the **sprit adjuster** about 5-8cm. This puts shape into the sail.
- Don't try to adjust the other controls.
- Sit in the same place as you did on the beat – with your front leg against the **midship beam**. But if the **bow** digs in to the water, move back.
- If a gust hits you, lean back and give a pull on the **mainsheet**. This is *pumping*.
- Take the **mainsheet** straight from the clip on the **boom**. It's much quicker to adjust the sail with a direct pull.
- Adjust the **mainsheet** so the sail flaps at the **luff**. Then pull in the mainsheet until the sail just stops flapping. **Telltales** (strips of wool or tape on each side of the sail) help here: adjust the sail until both telltales fly backwards. If the *windward telltale* (on the side of the sail nearer the wind) hangs down, pull in the mainsheet. If the *leeward telltale* (on the other side of the sail) hangs down, let out the mainsheet.

Reaching in light winds
- Move to sit a little further forward and heel (tip) the boat towards the wind slightly.
- Let off the **sprit** to put even more fullness into the sail.

Reaching in strong winds
- There is no chance of moving forward to let off the **sprit** in strong winds. Leave it as it was on the beat.
- Sit further back in the boat to lift the **bow**.
- Play the waves by moving your body. When the time comes to surf (plane) down a wave, lean out and back and pump the **mainsheet**.
- Look out for big gusts and try to turn away from the wind (bear away) before they hit you. Hike hard and pump the **mainsheet** to plane away from the gust before it has a chance to spin you round into the wind.

Going faster when running
- The **sprit** is the same as for reaching – as loose as possible without any creases in the sail.
- Pull up the **daggerboard** until none of it is in the water. (It is helpful to draw a line on the board to show you how far up it should be.)

Chapter 14 **How to go faster**

- Make sure there is a knot in the **mainsheet** to stop the **boom** going out further than a right angle to the boat. Let out the mainsheet to this knot, but keep the end of the rope in your hand.

Kiting

- Use your body weight to tip (*kite*) the boat to windward (towards the wind). To do this, sit on the **gunwale**, and grab the **toestrap** with your mainsheet hand. Lean back and pull the boat towards you.
- This reduces the amount of boat that's in the water, and causes the sail to be directly above the boat and higher, so you get more wind.
- But be careful not to tip too much! Stop when the water is running along the **gunwale**.
- If the boat rolls, pull in the **mainsheet** hard and move quickly towards the other (leeward) side.

Running in light winds

- In light winds, the **boom** may not stay out when you kite the boat, so use the paddle to hold it out.

Running in strong winds

- For speed, have the **daggerboard** up. (It's safer, but slower, to push it down halfway, as this helps to stop the boat rolling.)
- Pulling in the **mainsheet** also stops rolling, but slows you down.
- Sit well back to stop the **bow** nosediving. Keep the boat fairly flat – it is too dangerous to kite in strong winds.
- There is no chance of letting off the **sprit** – leave it tight.

15. What's next?

Once you've learnt the basic skills, the best way of getting more from sailing is to join a club. If you haven't yet bought a dinghy, you should be able to sail with other club members or borrow club boats. That will help you to choose the right class of dinghy.

If you already have a boat, the sailing club will give you a base for your sailing and provide an introduction to racing, if that's what you want.

To find details about sailing clubs, contact your national authority for the sport. In the UK, that's the Royal Yachting Association (www.rya.org.uk). They look after every aspect of sailing, from training schemes for beginners to advice and help for experienced sailors and clubs.

Before you join a club, visit several to see exactly what they offer junior sailors. A well-organised club will have special activities for young people, which could include:

- Basic training
- Weekend camps
- Barbecues
- Visits to other clubs
- Race training
- Summer camps
- Fun days
- Open weekends

The junior fleet leader will be able to tell you more.

Another way of finding the right club is to contact the class association of the boat you want to sail. Every good class of dinghy has a lively national association made up of the people who sail that design. The Optimist, for example, has class associations in 47 countries (www.optiworld.org). Each national association co-ordinates that country's club fleets (in the UK this is www.optimistsailing.org.uk).

For older sailors

When you move on from your first junior dinghy, exactly the same advice applies. If you can't decide what sort of boat will be best, your choice might be influenced by the fleets at your local

Chapter 15 What's next?

club, as it's obviously better to select a popular class.

Learning more
Apart from training courses at sailing schools and clubs, the best way of keeping in touch is by reading one of the many yachting magazines. Each one is aimed at a certain section of the sport, so you can choose the one which interests you most.

Many dinghy sailors learn more from the large number of books on the sport, and Fernhurst Books provide a range of titles covering sailing from start to finish.

One thing is certain – once you start sailing, you've got a sport which will keep you involved for life. Happy sailing!

Other books that will help

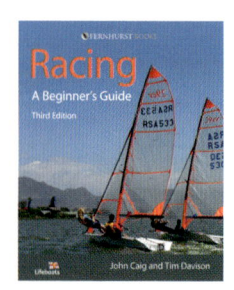

Taking your first steps into racing
Once you are confident sailing the boat, you will probably want to start racing it! *Racing: A Beginner's Guide* by John Caig & Tim Davison will give a flying start to your competitive sailing! It starts with the basics, and then takes you through rigging, training, tactics, strategy and tuning your boat.

Starting in a new class of boat
Choosing a class of boat to sail can be tricky, but once you have chosen the fun part is getting to know the boat and learning how to sail it really well! Why not try *The Mirror Book*, *The Topper Book* or *The Laser Book* to help make your decision, and get the most from your new boat.

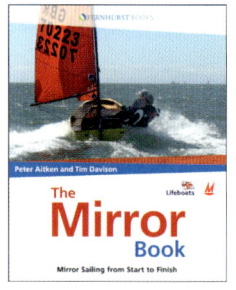

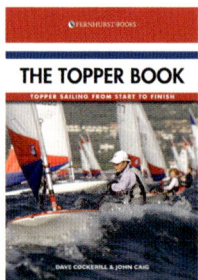

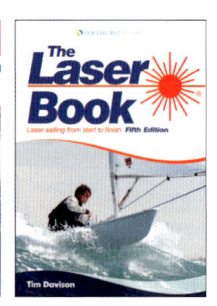

Taking your racing to the next level
Sail to Win is a series of fantastic guides for those who enjoy racing and want to work their way further up the leaderboard! Written by world class sailors and sailing coaches, these books will have you dazzling on the water in no time! Current titles in this series include *Helming to Win* by 'Champion of Champions' Nick Craig and *Coach Yourself to Win* by Olympic gold medal winning coach Jon Emmett.

For parents...

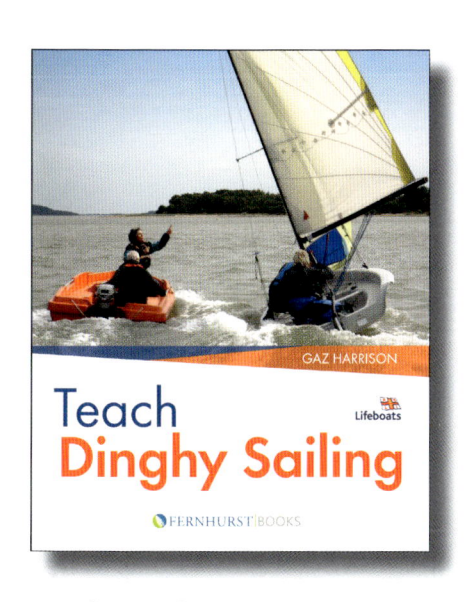

Teach Dinghy Sailing
by Gaz Harrison

A step-by-step guide on how to teach your children to sail safely and effectively. For each concept introduced there are off-the-water instructions as well as exercises to do once on the water, plus 'Top Tips' and 'Watch Out!' information. Help your child get the most from their boat, and begin their sailing journey with them!

www.fernhurstbooks.com